Bridges of the Dee and its Tributaries

Royal Deeside

W Stewart Wilson
Chris Engel

All profits from this book
will be donated to Alzheimer Scotland
www.alzscot.org

Cover Photo:
Old Bridge of Dee at Invercauld by Mike Stephen

Bridge Builder

An old man going a lone highway,
Came, at the evening cold and gray,
To a chasm vast and deep and wide.
Through which was flowing a sullen tide
The old man crossed in the twilight dim,
The sullen stream had no fear for him;
But he turned when safe on the other side
And built a bridge to span the tide.

'Old man,' said a fellow pilgrim near,
'You are wasting your strength with building here;
Your journey will end with the ending day,
You never again will pass this way;
You've crossed the chasm, deep and wide,
Why build this bridge at evening tide?'

The builder lifted his old gray head;
'Good friend, in the path I have come,' he said,
'There followed after me to-day
A youth whose feet must pass this way.
This chasm that has been as naught to me
To that fair-haired youth may a pitfall be;
He, too, must cross in the twilight dim;
Good friend, I am building this bridge for him!'

Will Allen Dromgoole (1900)

Contents

Foreword

A dictionary definition of a bridge might be *a structure carrying a road, path, railway etc across a river, road or other obstacle*. The reality is far more profound. Bridges facilitate travel, transportation and communication between places and people.

The Scottish landscape is generally hostile terrain over which to travel. Early populations travelled on water by rivers, lochs and the sea as is evidenced by flint tool distributions. As the need for travel along habitual routes increased, fords and ferries were established. The amazing, surviving Roman aqueducts across Europe suggest that the Romans may well have introduced bridge-building to Britain. However, there are few surviving British bridges predating the 1300s. The bridge of Balgownie on the River Don is the oldest in Scotland, having been built around 1310 - or possibly earlier.

This book describes bridges of Deeside from the early 1500s onwards and tells a fascinating story of endeavour, innovation and tenacity in overcoming the challenges of topography, climate and nature.

Notes

- The sequence of descriptions runs from source to sea and includes tributaries in the order of confluence with the Dee.
- Not every single bridge on Deeside has been included, only those where it has been possible to find historical information.
- Text in *italics* indicates words or sections that are being quoted or referenced.
- The written narrative uses metric units of measurement, but old, imperial and obsolete units have been preserved in quoted passages.
- Where possible, old monochrome photos have been used and have been coloured using digital image editing software. Where no old images are available, newer, colour photographs have been used within terms of the relevant Creative Commons Licenses.
- Some bridges mentioned in this book are on private land. If visiting, please be compliant with access restrictions and the Countryside Code.

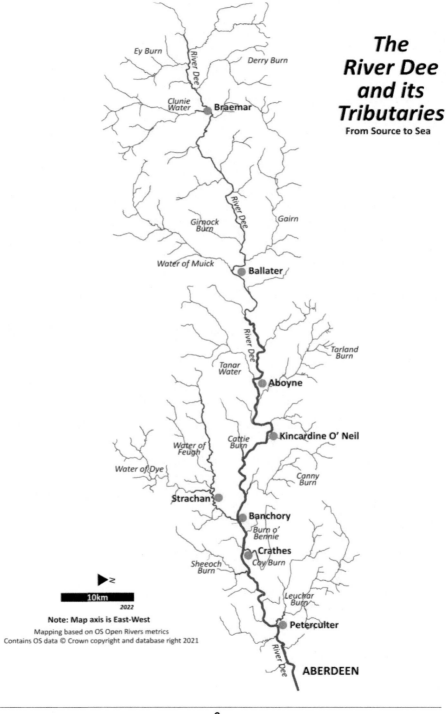

The River Dee and its Tributaries
From Source to Sea

Ey Burn

Derry Burn

River Dee

Clunie Water

Braemar

River Dee

Girnock Burn

Gairn

Water of Muick

Ballater

River Dee

Tarland Burn

Tanar Water

Aboyne

Kincardine O' Neil

Cattie Burn

Water of Feugh

Canny Burn

Water of Dye

Strachan

Banchory

Burn o' Bennie

Crathes

Sheeoch Burn

Coy Burn

Leuchar Burn

Peterculter

River Dee

ABERDEEN

N

10km

2022

Note: Map axis is East-West

Mapping based on OS Open Rivers metrics
Contains OS data © Crown copyright and database right 2021

Introduction

In AD 146 the Græco-Roman astronomer, Claudius Ptolemy, produced a map of Scotland for his *System of Geography*. He had never visited Scotland and had relied on information he had collected but he gave the river the name *Deva Fluvius* - (latin for river). Deva has the meaning *Goddess* which echoes that in medieval times the people believed that rivers had a divine being. The Romans left this part of Scotland in the early third century and the river later became known with the Gaelic name of: *Uisge Dhè* - the water of the Dee.

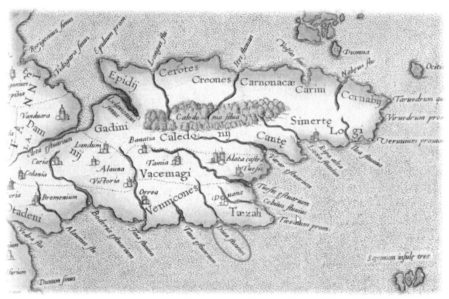

Detail from a map of 1584 based on Ptolemy's map of Britain (north to right)

Thomas Tennant in his *Tour of Scotland* in 1769 gives this account of his journey to Deeside:

I crossed the Dee near its head, which, from an insignificant stream, in the course of a few miles, increases to the size of a great river, from the influx of numbers of other waters; and is remarkable for continuing near fifty miles of its course, from Invercauld to within six miles of Aberdeen, without any sensible augmentation.

Heavy rain and melting snow can cause the river to become a raging torrent. Among the worst floods were those of 1769, 1920 and the Cairngorm floods of 1956, but they do not compare with the Muckle Spate of August 1829 which was almost surpassed by the havoc caused by Storm Frank in late December 2015.

Along the length of its south bank the river is overlooked by the Mounth, from the Gaelic *monadh* meaning mountain or moorland which shuts off Deeside from the south. It is crossed by nine major passes through which marauding armies have sought to invade the north. For centuries they have been the routes taken by travellers, cattle drovers, raiders and even the illicit whisky smugglers on the way south to Angus and Perthshire. The nine major crossings over the Mounth were:

> Cairnwell from Glenshee to Braemar
> Tolmounth from Glen Clova to Glen Callater
> Capel Mounth from Glen Clova to Glen Muick
> Fir Mounth from Tarfside to Glen Tanar
> Forest of Birse Mounth from Tarfside to Aboyne
> Cairn O' Mounth from Fettercairn to Kincardine O' Neil
> Cryne's Corse Mounth from Laurencekirk to Mills of Drum
> Elsick Mounth from Stonehaven to Drum
> Causey Mounth from Cowie to Aberdeen

The passes all led over the Grampians from the south and before any bridges were built the Dee required to be forded. The former Aberdeen City Librarian, G M Fraser, in his book *The Old Deeside Road*, published in 1921, listed 36 fords along the river recording that some were occasionally still used. In addition, he listed 27 ferries with three, the Inch ferry at Culter, the Heathcot ferry at Blairs and the one at Kincardine O' Neil still in use well into the twentieth century.

Prior to 1800 there were only four bridges across the river - the Bridge of Dee at Aberdeen (1527), the old Bridge at Invercauld (1752), the Bridge at Ballater (1799) and the one at Banchory (1799). The coming of the railway to Deeside on the north bank of the river, first to Banchory in 1853 and extended to Ballater in 1866, saw the need for new bridges to give access for passengers from the south. By 1921 Fraser lists 24 but many have seen changes or been totally rebuilt in the last one hundred years. Three completely new bridges have been added - the King George VI and Queen Elizabeth bridges serving the new housing and industrial developments in the suburbs of Aberdeen and most recently the bridge at Maryculter carrying traffic on Aberdeen's peripheral road. Another bridge which is no longer and not mentioned by Fraser but is listed in Fenton Wyness's authoritative book *Royal Valley*, published in 1968, is Stewart's Bridge at Banchory-Devenick.

Along the course of the Dee, the river is joined by 17 major tributaries, the largest being the Lui, Clunie, Muick, Tanar and Feugh.

Some of the older bridges of the Dee and the tributaries are category A-listed, that is, they are of national or international importance, because of their architectural or historic significance. The A-listed bridges, with dates of completion in brackets are Brunel's bridge at Balmoral (1859), Crathie suspension bridge (1834), Potarch (1814), Park (1854), Bridge of Dee in Aberdeen (1527) and Wellington suspension bridge (1830). In addition, two bridges on tributaries of the river are also A-listed, Gairnshiel (1753) and Bridge of Dye (1680). The other stone and suspension bridges are category B - examples of bridges of regional or local importance.

The first visit of Queen Victoria to Deeside was in 1848 and she wrote *all seemed to breathe freedom and peace and to make us forget the world and its turmoils.* In June 1852 the old castle and estate of Balmoral was bought by Prince Albert who replaced it with the castle we know today. He also commissioned two bridges, one at Balmoral (1857) and the other at Invercauld (1859). In 1868 the Queen wrote about her *dear Paradise* in her *Journal of our Life in the Highlands* and told the world about its delights. The Royal family's love for this part of Scotland continues to this day and has allowed the valley to earn the name Royal Deeside.

The Royal Burgh of Aberdeen lies between two rivers, the Dee and the Don. Joseph Robertson, the Scottish historian, writing in 1843, described the Dee as a *pretty clear river; shallow and somewhat quick, running much on gravel and having several fords: but after it rains it becomes very big and impetuous.*

He goes on to compare the two rivers:

> *A mile of Don's worth two of Dee*
> *Except for salmon, stone and tree*

The Dee was once a plentiful river for salmon. In the book *Description of the East Coast of Scotland* by F Douglas published in 1782, he writes on the abundance of salmon caught on the Dee: *the take is reckoned to afford yearly about seventy last of salmon.* A last is an old Scottish measure for twelve barrels with each barrel containing about 113 kg (250 pounds) of fish. It is said that some servants on Deeside had contracts limiting the number of times they were served salmon in a week!

The river follows a course of over 137 km to the North Sea at Aberdeen - initially dropping 610 metres into Glen Dee and becoming one of the fastest flowing rivers in Scotland. Fenton Wyness in his book, *Royal Valley,* comments that *although the Dee is neither the longest nor the grandest river in Scotland, it is surely one of the most fascinating and picturesque.* The bridges of the Dee and its many tributaries are, in their own way, fascinating and picturesque and have made a significant contribution to the history of Royal Deeside.

The Sources of the Dee

The Dee has two sources, the Garchary and Larig burns. Near the summit of Braeraiach, at a height of 1240 metres, two small streams of clear water emerge to form a number of pools called the Wells of Dee. From there the burn is called the Garchary; it flows east across the level ground to the Falls of Dee where the burn plunges into An Garbh Choire - *the burn of the rough corrie.* Another stream, the Larig, rises from the Pools of Dee at a height of 820 metres between Braeriach and Ben Macdhui and flows south down the Lairig Ghru for about 2.5 km to join the Garchary. The united stream becomes the river we know as the Dee.

The first bridge it meets is a footbridge leading to Corrour Bothy. Before 1959 the crossing was but a simple structure consisting of suspended steel wires between posts on either bank and was especially dangerous when the river was in spate. The Dee is then joined by the Geusachan burn from the west. Glen Dee, through which the young river flows, is both narrow and rugged and is followed until it reaches the Chest of Dee and the White Bridge, dating from 1881, but rebuilt in 1908. There the Geldie Burn joins the river which then turns east until it reaches the Linn of Dee, the first of many vehicular bridges.

There has been much debate on which of the two sources is the more dominant. Dr Hill Burton in his book *Cairngorm Mountains* published in 1864 elected for the Larig, *as less desperately flighty, more voluminous, and more in the line of the glen*, than the Garchary. Today, however, it is accepted that the Garchary is the principal source because of its longer descent and rising at a higher altitude.

Metal bridge over the Corrour

The White Bridge

The Linn of Dee

There have been various crossings of the gorge, the first being a single plank across the gorge and later by a structure described as an *alpine timber bridge but known to locals as an auld, rickety, widden brig.* Sir Thomas Dick Lauder in his book *The Great Moray Floods of 1829*, but with chapters on the River Dee, describes the bridge as *thrown, for the passage of carts, at a height of 30 feet across the stream.* It was washed away in the great flood of 1829 when the flood rose nearly a metre above the bridge. It was replaced by another wooden bridge which survived until the present bridge was built in 1857. It was the work of W Reid and was commissioned by James, 5th Earl of Fife.

The bridge was opened on Tuesday 8 September by Queen Victoria. It is described *as a large Gothic single-span bridge, built of squared and coursed pink granite, with bull-faced granite to the side piers.* The parapet is stepped and on the east is a blank cartouche which formerly depicted the arms of the Earls of Fife. On the west is an inscription marking the opening in 1857.

Queen Victoria gave an account of the opening in her diary:

Balmoral
September 8, 1857

At half-past one o'clock we started in "Highland state," Albert in a royal Stuart plaid, and I and the girls in skirts of the same, with the ladies (who had returned at five in the morning from the ball at Mar Lodge) and gentlemen, for the Linn of Dee, to open the new bridge there. The valley looked beautiful. A triumphal arch was erected at which Lord Fife and Mr. Brooke received us, and walked near the carriage. pipers playing, the road lined with Duff men. On the bridge Lady Fife received us, and we drank in whisky prosperity to the bridge. The view of the Linn is very fine from it. All the company and a band were outside a tent on the bank overlooking the bridge. Here we took some tea, talked with the company, and then drove back to the Mar Lodge. The Fifes preceding us to the end of the grounds. We were home at half-past five, not without having some rain by the way.

She was to visit this spot many times on her visits to Balmoral and on 7 October 1873 her daughter, Princess Beatrice, was with her. In her journal entry of that day, she describes how they *lunched in the usual place, near the Linn and then sketched, but I was terribly tormented by midges.* Nothing changes!

Lady Jaffray, who lived at Edgehill in Milltimber, recalls on a visit in 1929 seeing the rough-hewn granite stone marking the spot where a girl had drowned some seven years before. At the time she mentions there was a notice, near the fire warning of the Forestry Commission, written in doggerel verse which still has a message for us today as we enjoy the beauty of this special spot.

Banana skins and luncheon scraps
Orange peel and chocolate wraps,
Broken bottles, torn rags,
Kodak cases, paper bags,
Cigarettes and matches spent,
Cardboard plates and papers rent,
Smashed cups and empty tins
Spoil the beauty of the Linns

Bridges of the Lui

Metal bridge on upper part of the Lui

Glen Lui is one of the major glens on the Mar Lodge estate. The Lui Water is a tributary of the Dee formed by the meeting of the Derry burn with the Luibeg burn. It joins the Dee less than a kilometre downstream from the Linn of Dee.

Luibeg Bridge and Bothy

The road bridge was built on solid rock, the foundations being at some height above the surface when the river is in its normal state. In the floods of 1829, we are told that a cavern was cut out in the rock under the north-east abutment large enough for a man to shelter in.

Lui road bridge

The Canadian Bridge

The Canadian Bridge

At the outbreak of World War II, Britain was almost wholly dependent on imports of timber to supply her needs. The country had timber but the war had robbed the country of the manpower to fell the trees.

Experienced Canadian loggers came to Scotland and took over the job of felling the timber to help in the war effort. They set up their camps at various places on Deeside - at Blackhall in Banchory, Ballater, Aboyne and Mar Lodge. The camp at Mar Lodge was situated where the Lui joins the Dee. Over two hundred men from Company 25 were stationed there from March 1942 to June 1944. The Canadian Bridge, as it became known, was constructed by the loggers over the River Dee and was ready for use by the end of August 1942.

An article, written in 2018, by Katy Fennema for the *Braemar Highland Experience* explains in detail some of the work of the loggers:

The felling of trees was just a small part of their work. The subsequent trimming was more difficult, and the transportation particularly challenging on steep hillsides and poor roads. Once the trees were taken off the hillside, they were dumped in a manmade ditch 10 feet deep and 20 feet wide before being sawn. This had two benefits, as it rid the logs of dirt and also made them easier to manoeuvre onto the machinery that took the logs to the sawmill. Once sawn into boards, a light railway was then used to take the timber via a bridge to trucks waiting at Inverey.

From there the timber was taken to Ballater and then by rail to Aberdeen. The bridge the Canadians built over the River Dee was intended only as a temporary structure but it survived until possibly 1963 when floods undermined its foundations. The bridge had been so well constructed that its demolition proved to be difficult.

The Bridge of Ey

Road bridge over the Ey Burn

The Ey burn rises near the boundary of Aberdeenshire and Angus and flows northwards through Glen Ey and is joined by the Allt Connie burn before it joins the Dee at Inverey. In 1798, Inverey was added to Mar Estate by James Duff, 2nd Earl of Fife.

The bridge, a single arch bridge, links Muckle and Little Inverey and was built by the Mar estate around 1799. It replaced an earlier crossing which is shown on a map of 1743 and it is said to have cost £50. John Farquharson of Inverey had a castle at Inverey and is often referred to as the Black Colonel. He took part in the Jacobite rising of 1689 and to prevent Government troops occupying Braemar Castle he burnt it to the ground.

The Battle of Killiecrankie, in 1689, was a Jacobite victory but the uprising was soon at an end and he returned to his castle. Pursued by Government troops he evaded capture by taking shelter further up Glen Ey on a shelf of rock known to this day as The Colonel's Bed.

Victoria Bridge at Mar Lodge Estate

Victoria Bridge, Mar Lodge Estate

An account written in 1848 gives an interesting description of the estate. It describes the location of Mar Lodge, in the bottom of the valley, *as a commodious hunting-seat of the Earl of Fife's and that it was being rented, with the adjoining deer forests, by the Duke of Leeds*. It was during his tenancy of the estate, which lasted for twenty years, that the wooden bridge was built which replaced one which was destroyed in the Muckle Spate of 1829. The Mar Lodge at that time was behind the present Mar Lodge and had been bought by the then Earl of Fife in the eighteenth century. Queen Victoria laid the foundation stone of the present Lodge in 1895, built for Princess Louise, her grand-daughter, and her husband the Duke of Fife. It was completed in 1898.

Fraser's Bridge in Glen Clunie

The authors of *The Buildings of Scotland Aberdeenshire South and Aberdeen* suggest that the initials and dates of 1862/1863 on the parapet refer to masons carrying out repairs to the road instigated by Prince Albert. The bridge is still in use today for light traffic.

Coldrach Bridge

The Braemar Wrights Society dates back to 1815. In 1826 it became the Braemar Highland Society which in 1866 had Royal added to its name. It is known the world over for the Braemar Gathering, now held each year on the first Saturday of September. Wrights Societies were common all over Scotland and were a form of Mutual Benefit or Friendly Society owned by the members, whereby needy members could be given financial help if required.

In the 2015 *Braemar Gathering Annual*, John Duff recounts that *in the early years of the society the vrichts or wrights assembled in their white aprons on a pre-arranged day in late summer to form a procession, headed by a piper, through Auchendryne, then south along the old military road to Coldrach, where they crossed the Clunie and returned via what was known as the Laird's Ride to the old Market Stance in Castleton.* On reaching Castleton the wrights engaged in some athletic sports, the forerunner of the Games of today.

Coldrach Bridge, near Braemar   *Aug 1905.*
Mrs Connon & And.

The bridge at Coldrach is remembered in a verse from Professor John
Stuart Blackie's Braemar ballads:

<blockquote>
Coldrach Bridge,
Where the forceful mountain current
Cuts through the pointed granite ledge
With deep, dark, swirling current.
</blockquote>

It was not until Queen Victoria's arrival to Balmoral and with the
enthusiasm of Prince Albert and the then Farquharson clan chief, that work
started on a new road replacing the old Laird's Ride. Neither were to live
long enough to see the work completed in 1864. The road is now part of
the A93.

Braemar Golf Course Bridge

The nine hole course dates from 1902 and came into use the following
year. Much of the course lay alongside the River Clunie. In 1911 the Club
was given ground across the Clunie allowing the course to be extended to
18 holes. The Club had a great benefactor in Lord William James Pirrie,
who became 1st Viscount Pirrie in 1921. He was a leading businessman
and chairman of Harland & Wolff, the shipyard in Belfast that built the ill-
fated Titanic.

Bridge on Braemar golf course

Lord Pirrie was a keen golfer and had a private nine hole course in the grounds of Ormiston House, his home in Belfast. He was also a frequent visitor to Braemar, staying each summer in the first floor suite at the Fife Arms Hotel which had undergone major reconstruction in the late 1890s. He enjoyed playing the course and was elected Captain in 1910 - 11. He not only financed much of the cost of the extension to the Braemar course but personally supervised the work, including the building of the substantial bridge allowing access to the additional holes across the Clunie.

It is reported that by 1993 the bridge had bordered on the unsafe for years even decades and a much wider bridge was built as a replacement.

Society Bridge in Braemar

In 1953 the Braemar Royal Highland Society built a footbridge as a link from a car park off the A93 to the games park. The bridge, we are told, was built at a cost of £236. 14s. 2d but was washed away by ice a few years later and it was not until October 2005 that the new Society bridge was built across the Clunie. It was opened by Prince Charles, Duke of Rothesay. The new one, costing in the region of £28,000, was funded by Scottish Natural Heritage and the European Union.
The project, initiated by Braemar Community Council, was constructed to plans commissioned by Aberdeenshire Council. The project was taken over by the Upper Deeside Access Trust and has been incorporated into an extended path network around the village.

Society Bridge over the Clunie Water in Braemar

Bridge over the Clunie Water in Braemar

Before the eleventh century, there were separate hamlets on each bank of the Clunie, Auchendryne on the west and Castleton on the east. Castleton refers to Kindrochit Castle, located within the modern village, rather than Braemar Castle. Malcolm III came to the area in around 1059 and built a timber bridge connecting the east and west banks. Kindrochit means *bridge end* and the castle was of immense strategic importance guarding routes from the south. It was a favourite summer residence of King Robert II who used the Cairnwell or Tolmounth on his journeys to the castle.

Over the years there have been many crossings at this point. By 1832 the then bridge was considered to be very narrow and thirty years later, in 1862, it was reported that the bridge was in a dangerous state. James Duff, the 5th Earl of Fife and James Farquharson, the 12th laird of Invercauld initially funded the cost of a replacement with the road trustees *refunding such instalments for the next ten years as the trustees think fit*

The bridge was completed by 1863 but widened more than once in the twentieth century.

Bridge over the Clunie Water in Braemar

Old Bridge of Dee at Invercauld

The old Bridge of Dee crosses the River Dee near Invercauld. It dates back to 1753 and was built by Major Caulfeild. It was part of the military road to link Blairgowrie with Corgarff and Inverness. The intention of Caulfeild's road was to ensure that there could never be another Jacobite Rising. For more than 80 years after it was built, a garrison remained at Braemar Castle to ensure that Jacobite sympathisers did not get up to any seditious activities. This section of the road was built by four companies of Holm's Regiment of Foot, two of Lord George Beauclerk's and one of Lt Gen Shelton's. The bridge was not aligned to the military road, but to the road travelling westwards through the Ballochbuie Forest. Originally it consisted of three arches all of different sizes. Later the bridge was lengthened with two flood arches on the north approach and one on the south. The cutwaters (a wedge-shaped projection on the pier of a bridge, which divides the flow of water to prevent debris from becoming trapped) were also additions and served as buttresses.

Caulfeild had to do extensive blasting of rock to enable its construction, causing injury to men and a fatal accident was reported on 24 July 1753 in the *Aberdeen Journal*. This rubble bridge with solid parapet is one of the oldest bridges crossing the Dee and withstood the Muckle Spate of 1829. In 1973 the bridge came into the care of Historic Environment Scotland. That year some excavation work was undertaken and again some seven years later, revealing an earlier cobbled surface. Over the years the bridge has been regularly inspected and repaired as necessary.

Invercauld Bridge

The old main road through Deeside ran along the south side of the river between Ballater and Braemar, with the Old Bridge of Dee connecting to the military road which crossed from the north bank. However, the road ran very close to Queen Victoria's Balmoral castle and concerned about her privacy she, or perhaps more precisely, her Government, approved the new Turnpike Act in 1855 which saw a new road built along the north bank of the river. This road required the building of a new bridge across the Dee leading to Braemar. This was built at the expense of Prince Albert. The builder was J F Beattie and the design may be that of William Smith, who had worked on the new Balmoral. When completed in 1859 it allowed the Road Trustees to close the road over the old bridge.

The following notice was displayed for the next 60 years, closing the road through Balmoral estate:

PUBLIC NOTICE
THE TRUSTEES OF THE BALLATER TURNPIKE ROAD
HEREBY GIVE NOTICE THAT THIS ROAD IS CLOSED
AND
DECLARED A PRIVATE ROAD. SEPT., 1859.

The new stretch of North Deeside Road left an interesting problem for the lodge on the north bank of the river close to the old bridge. Originally a lodge for the entrance to Invercauld House it was now marooned, so Queen

Victoria bought the ground surrounding it and also the house as a lodge for a private entrance to Balmoral. The house was known locally as *Threepenny-Bit Cottage* – its 12-sided shape being similar to a pre-decimal threepenny coin.

In September 2018 one way traffic on the bridge had to be introduced for a short time, to allow engineers to undertake investigation of structural defects. It was so timed to ensure minimal inconvenience for traffic travelling to that year's Braemar Gathering.

Danzig Suspension Bridge (Ballochbuie Bridge)

A short distance downriver is the private Danzig suspension footbridge built in 1924 by James Abernethy & Co. The name needs some explanation. When in 1866 the Deeside railway was extended to Ballater the plan had been to extend the line to Braemar. The route to Braemar would have passed close to Balmoral Castle but this was abandoned in May 1865 when Queen Victoria objected, wishing the upper part of the Dee Valley to be preserved as a natural Highland region. By 1868 the ground from Ballater to Bridge of Gairn was being prepared for the goods railway intended to carry timber from Ballochbuie forest, then owned by Col James Farquharson of Invercauld, the 13th laird.

Without much warning, construction on the line was halted. That year the forest was leased for ten years by Queen Victoria and bought outright by her on 15 May 1878 to prevent it being bought for the felling of its timber. To mark this significant event, the Queen had a cairn erected on the Balmoral Estate with the inscription:

QUEEN VICTORIA ENTERED INTO
POSSESSION OF THE
BALLOCHBUIE 15th MAY 1878.
THE BONNIEST PLAID IN SCOTLAND

The Bonniest Plaid in Scotland recalls the old legend that McGregor, the last laird of Ballochbuie, sold the forest to Farquharson of Invercauld for a tartan plaid.

Not far from the Danzig bridge, there had been an old sawmill of that name. It is not known whether the mill was owned by a Danziger or if the mill owners had a business in the city of Danzig. The Queen lost no time after her acquisition of Ballochbuie to start building on the site of the old mill, a retreat which she named Danzig Shiel. It was completed by June 1882 and used regularly by the Queen for the rest of her reign. It was her favourite place to go and enjoy afternoon tea and entertain her guests. During World War I, because of the rise of the anti-German feeling, there was an attempt to change the name but without success and it was not until the beginning of World War II that the name was changed to the Garbh Allt Shiel.

Garrawalt Bridge

The Garbh Allt burn, now spelt Garrawalt, rises on Lochnagar and tumbles down through the Ballochbuie forest to the falls of Garrawalt before reaching the Dee. The footbridge over the falls replaced an earlier wooden one which was described by James Brown in his book *The New Deeside Guide* published in 1862, as *a very curious wooden bridge, which has few matches for elegance and curiosity of structure.* The present bridge was built in 1878 by Blaikie Bros, engineers of Aberdeen. The decorative green wrought iron bridge is of a most pleasing design and it has been suggested that it *would not be out of place in a park or estate garden.*

Garrawalt Bridge

Since the days of Queen Victoria this has been a favourite picnic spot for the Royal family. In September 1971 the waterfall was the background for a photograph showing Her Majesty sitting on rocks with two of her corgis. It was taken as one of a series to mark her Silver Wedding celebrations in 1972.

Feardar Burn

The Feardar burn on the north side of the Dee is a tributary which joins the river near Crathie. It derives its name from the Gaelic *Feuardur* meaning the stream of the grassy glen. The remote glens of upper Deeside had been for centuries the ideal place for the illegal distilling of whisky and the people of the area banded together to thwart the best efforts of the excisemen who were constantly on the lookout for the practice. The Excise Act of 1823 made distilling legal and spirit taxes were introduced. The first legal distillery may well have been built in Glen Feardar by James Robertson who at one time had been an illegal distiller. He was not popular with those who continued the practice and it is said that they retaliated by setting fire to his building. Undeterred, he rebuilt his distillery, calling it Lochnagar, but it met a similar fate. His third survived but was never a great success and was finally closed in 1860.

Bridges at Balmoral

Balmoral Suspension Bridge

In 1834 the only crossing of the Dee at Balmoral was by a suspension bridge which was completed that year. It replaced the ferry of Clachanturn, near Crathie. The bridge was the work of J Justice Junior & Co of Dundee. The bridge was particularly slim-looking. The builders were proud of their work and had their inscription on four places on the bridge:

J. JUSTICE JUNR. & CO.,
DUNDEE,
1834

The bridge had been built by Sir Robert Gordon who, in 1830, had acquired the lease of Balmoral from James Duff, 2nd Earl of Fife. Sir Robert died in 1847 and the lease passed to his older brother the 4th Earl of Aberdeen. In February of the following year, Prince Albert took over the lease without ever seeing the property. The Queen did not favour the bridge, preferring to use the crossing at Ballater.

The old suspension bridge was given some new life when in 1885 it was almost entirely rebuild by Blaikie Brothers of Aberdeen at the expense of the Queen. It was by that time only used as a footbridge. In November 1976 it was designated a category A structure and in 1989 the timber deck was replaced.

The Brunel Bridge

In 1852 Prince Albert bought Balmoral estate from the trustees of the Earl of Fife and the decision was taken to replace the small castle, which had been built by Sir Robert Gordon, by the one we know today. This was completed by 1855 but a bridge was required to link with the North Deeside Road. He admired the engineering genius of Isambard Kingdom Brunel who had designed the Crystal Palace for the Great Exhibition of 1851.

In the autumn of 1854 Prince Albert invited Brunel and his wife Mary to Balmoral. Brunel inspected the suspension bridge and his advice was - *I believe you may consider it perfectly safe for all ordinary loads tho' quite unfit to bear a crowd of people or a drove of cattle.* He recommended a possible site for a new bridge and made a few sketches before returning to Aberdeen and his train journey south. He later remarked, *didn't have time to stay with Queen Victoria.* In his report to Prince Albert, he said that his plan for the bridge was *the cheapest and most easily erected bridge and recommend it.*

With the design chosen, tenders were issued for the work and in 1856 the contract was awarded to R Brotherhood Railway Works of Chippenham, Wiltshire.

The build was supervised by Dr Andrew Robertson, the factor of Balmoral. The cost was £1550 and the work was completed by 1857. The structure sits on umbrella shaped girders so that rainwater would run off the wrought ironwork rather than lying and causing corrosion, so adding considerably to the life of the structure. The bridge was disliked by Queen Victoria and her displeasure seems to have been shared by others. G M Fraser, in his book *The Old Deeside Road*, says little about this bridge and even Fenton Wyness, in his book *Royal Valley*, fails to mention Brunel. Brunel was proud of his design and described it as *a fine example of functional elegance*. It remains a fine, though minor, example of his work and in May 1994 was given a category A-listing as a bridge of historic interest.

The Brunel bridge over the Dee at Balmoral

In April 2006, to commemorate the 200th anniversary of the birth of Brunel, his sketchbook showing two drawings for the proposed bridge was put on show in the ballroom of Balmoral Castle. It shows that he had submitted two possible designs for the structure. One was a smaller scale version of his famous Royal Albert bridge over the River Tamar in south-west England, but it was the second that was chosen - a wrought iron girder bridge. Both sketches are dated 18 December 1854.

On 29 May HRH The Duke of Edinburgh unveiled a plaque on the bridge which for the first time made mention of its designer.
In 2014 the bridge was closed for several months to carry out essential maintenance work. Initially, the work was scheduled for the summer but with the possibility that the bridge was used for roosting bats at that time, the work was postponed

until October, thus avoiding the Queen having to make a 32 km detour to reach the north bank of the river. The aged timber road surface was replaced, at a cost of around £400,000, by reinforced concrete and the bridge was repainted in its traditional dark green colour giving it many more years of service.

Abergeldie Bridge

Originally there was a rope and cable bridge across the river which was described as a heavy cable wound round a windlass on both banks and on it ran the Cradle, with two grooved wheels. The Cradle was only three planks held by iron hoops and curved like cradle rockers. On both ends there was an upright, joined by a cross-bar. The seating was for two and the cradle was usually worked by the Abergeldie Castle gardener. George Brown lived at Greystone across the river from Abergeldie Castle. He was a well-educated man and was a skilled weaver. He had a fairly large family but only one daughter.

The bridge was the scene of a tragic accident in 1824, when the rope broke and a young couple were drowned. The couple were Peter Frankie, a gamekeeper at Allt-na-giubhsaich and his bride was George Brown's daughter, Barbara, known to all her friends as Babby and because of her beauty, as the Flower of Deeside.

The tragic story is related in John Grant Michie's book Deeside Tales published in 1872 and also in an account written by Margaret Gordon who had married a son of George Brown, who was also named George:

The marriage took place in 1824 and the couple stayed a few days with Babby's father until the keeper's house was renovated. On the day of the tragedy, a Sunday, Babby and Peter were invited to the Smart's at Abergeldie Mains. Early in the afternoon they left George Brown's house and crossed the Dee. The water was high but not in spate. After the couple had spent a happy afternoon they left the Castle side of the river about 9 pm. By that time the water was higher. It appears that there was a fault with the windlass and the rope broke, throwing both occupants into the river. It was a dark night and people, including old George, searched the river bank with burning torches. It was not until daybreak that Babby's body was found, while Frankie was found a week later at Coilacriech. The whole of Deeside seemed to be in mourning.

This simple ropeway system was also used to carry mail and goods to the castle and it was the inspiration for John Fyffe, of Kemnay Quarries, to invent what he called a Blondin named after Charles Blondin, the famous tightrope walker. Fyffe used the idea to construct a suspension cableway with travelling carrier which was capable of lifting up to 20 tons of stone from the floor of the quarry to the top edge.

On 30 May 1885 a press report records that *the cradle bridge which has been used for nearly a century to carry passengers across the Dee at Abergeldie Castle, and over which the Prince and Princes of Wales and their children have travelled hundreds of times has been removed, and in its stead a handsome footbridge has been opened.*

Abergeldie suspension bridge

The suspension footbridge which links Abergeldie castle with the north bank of the Dee was built in 1885 by Blaikie Brothers, engineers of Aberdeen at the expense of Queen Victoria for the benefit of her guests using the Castle. Abergeldie was the summer residence of the Prince of Wales, later King Edward VII. The foundation was laid early in 1885 and the bridge was ready for use in time for his family's summer visit to Deeside. 1885 was the year of royal bridges; the bridge at Ballater was completed and opened by Queen Victoria on 6 November and also in the same year she had the suspension bridge at Crathie virtually rebuilt.

By 2005 the suspension bridge was in a poor state of repair and was declared unsafe to use. In the storms of December 2015 part of the embankment was washed away and the castle was in danger of being lost to the swollen River Dee. The castle was saved but the suspension footbridge did not survive.

The Birks of Aberfeldie is a song which Robert Burns composed on a visit in 1787 to the Falls of Moness at Aberfeldy. The original song *The Birks of Abergeldie* first appeared in manuscript in 1694 with the chorus which Burns used changing *Abergeldie* to *Aberfeldie*:

> *Bonie lassie, will you go,*
> *Will you go, will you go?*
> *Bonie lassie, will ye go*
> *To the birks of Abergeldie.*

Polhollick Bridge

Polhollick suspension bridge

Alexander Gordon was born in 1818 at Littlemill. He was a great benefactor to Ballater including meeting the cost of the Polhollick suspension footbridge built in 1892 which replaced the ferry. The pier for the old ferry and the former ferryman's house can still be seen. The bridge was the work of James Abernethy & Co. of Ferryhill in Aberdeen.

On the pillar of the bridge is the following inscription:

THIS BRIDGE
WAS PRESENTED
TO THE PUBLIC BY
MR. ALEXANDER GORDON,
SOUTHWOOD,
HILDENBOROUGH, KENT
ERECTED 1892

It was badly damaged on 16 November 1942 when a Whitley VP 5105 bomber, while on a flight from Kinloss, had engine failure and smashed into the bridge. Two of the five crew lost their lives. In 2020 a local man, who had emigrated to Australia, recalled that his two older brothers had been cycling home to Glen Girnock from Ballater and had crossed the bridge shortly before the plane crashed. One of his brothers ran back to Foot o' Gairn to report the accident and to get help.

By 2015 the bridge had a weight limit of four persons at any one time. Repairs were undertaken between May and October that year but in December the bridge was badly damaged by Storm Frank. The bridge was closed again and it was finally reopened in December 2018 allowing it to be used once again as part of the popular Seven Bridges walk around Ballater.

The Girnock Burn

The Girnock Burn, the noisy or gurgling stream, rises in hills to the south of the River Dee and flows northwards through Glen Girnock to join the Dee at Ballhaloch between Ballater and Crathie. The present stone bridge is on the south Deeside road not far from where the burn meets the Dee. There was an earlier bridge and the story of it is told in John Grant Michie's book Deeside Tales published in 1872.

Gordon of Knock and Forbes of Strathgirnock were bitter enemies. Forbes wanted to build a bridge across the Girnock to get to his peat moss but Gordon refused to allow any Forbes men to be on his land. Forbes said he would do it anyway and one day his men cut down some big trees and made a *brig o' logs*. Gordon was not happy and his men *threw it a down the burn*, but he came up with a challenge - *Next time ye try on a brig, ye can take advantage of the nicht time, and man for man, next day we'll send*

A suspension footbridge bridge across the Muick was built at Birkhall in 1880 for the Prince of Wales, later to be King Edward VII. The bridge used the tensioning system developed by an Aberdeen engineer, John Harper, and used specifically by his company in its bridge construction. On Saturday 19 June 1880 the *Aberdeen People's Journal* reported that *on the site of this bridge or near to it, no less than eight bridges have been erected during the last thirty-two years - since the estate was purchased by the late Prince Consort. The whole of the former bridges, which were made of wood, were either carried away by excessive floods or heavy gales which come down the valley of Glenmuick. The erection was superintended by Mr. Harper, senior, of Seafield, whose experience enabled him, with three men, to complete the whole structure in the remarkably short space of a week.*

The cost of the bridge was under £100.

It was washed away in the storms of December 2015. Douglas Harper, great-grandson of John, reminds us in his book *River, Railway and Ravine* that it had been the last remaining bridge designed and built by John Harper.

Prince Charles, Duke of Rothesay, inherited Birkhall from Queen Elizabeth, The Queen Mother, upon her death in 2002. He was devastated by the amount of damage done to the gardens of his estate and turned his attention to repairing the damage and restoring the footbridge. The contractor was able to use 75% of the original allowing it to be back in use by the summer of 2016. Once again it allows access to an arboretum planted in 2013 on what had been a piece of vacant land.

In an interview for the BBC in October 2021 Prince Charles said, *the great thing was that I managed to plant it the same year that my grandson was born, the eldest, George, so I thought I'd call it Prince George's wood.*

Bridge of Muick

W Douglas Simpson, in an article he wrote in 1928 for the *Society of Antiquaries of Scotland,* suggests that there might have been a medieval bridge at Invermuick. The evidence comes from a footnote in a book *Antiquities of the Shires of Aberdeen and Banff* by Dr George Grub published in 1847. He wrote: *The remains of a third bridge over the same river, probably of the same age, were lately brought to light near the mouth of Glenmuick.* The other two, referred to by Dr Grub, were at Kincardine O' Neil and the precursor of Bishop Dunbar's bridge in Aberdeen.

The present bridge was built around 1740 with a parapet dating from 1878. The bridge links Glen Muick south of the river to the old Invermuick parish church to the north. It is close to where the Muick meets the Dee and is reminiscent of military bridges of the period but there is no evidence it was built as such.

Close by there is an interesting cairn marking the spot where, on 16 September 1899, Queen Victoria while driving met by chance, the 1st Battalion Gordon Highlanders who were in camp at Glen Muick. Two days later the battalion was presented with new colours by The Prince of Wales, later to be King Edward VII. Only a month later they were mobilised and arrived in South Africa to play a significant role in the Boer War.

Ballater Bridge

In the early part of the eighteenth century attempts were made to replace the ford and ferry at Ballater with a bridge but without success until 1776. The bridge was funded from many sources - private subscription, the board of forfeited and annexed estates set up after the 1745 Jacobite rising, the Farquharsons and other local landowners. A bridge of stone was built about 100m east of this site in 1783 and was swept away by flood in 1799. A second bridge of stone was built by Telford 20m east of this site in 1809 and was swept away by floods in 1829.

A vivid account of the destruction of this is given in Sir Thomas Dick Lauder's book *The Great Moray Floods of 1829.* In the chapter on the River Dee he writes: *The rain and hurricane on the 3rd of August was attended, in the evening, by the brightest lightning, and the loudest thunder, ever seen or heard there.* The account goes on to mention that Ballater was crowded with invalids and other visitors brought together by the healing powers of the nearby Pannanich Wells.

It is said that the wells were discovered some time in the mid eighteenth century when an old sick woman, Elspet or Isabella Michie, who suffered from scrofula, sometimes known as the *King's Evil,* a form of tuberculosis, bathed in the muddy pools and drank the spa waters. Gradually the old woman's health improved and soon news of the miracle cure spread. But the destruction was not over and the following morning at *half past 3 o'clock, the flood increased, and swept before it the two northern arches of the bridge at one and the same instant; and, in the course of two hours afterwards, the three others were borne away in succession. Those who saw the first arches go, assured me that the noise was tremendous, and that the splash of the water was so great that it was driven over the tops of the adjoining houses.*

Those caught up in the flood were lucky not to drown and had fortunately moved, prior to the worst of the flooding, to find a dry house on the higher ground of the village.

The ferry boat was brought back into use until 1834 when it was replaced by a wooden bridge which lasted till 6 November 1885, when the present bridge, built by County Road Trustees, was opened by Queen Victoria who named it *The Royal Bridge - Long may it stand.*

1834-1885 wooden bridge at Ballater

1885 Stone bridge at Ballater

When in the mid 1990s the plaque was beginning to become illegible, a restored plaque was made and was unveiled by Her Majesty Queen Elizabeth on 8 September 1998 but unfortunately it contains an error. The date given for the destruction of the bridge erected in 1783 is given as 1789.

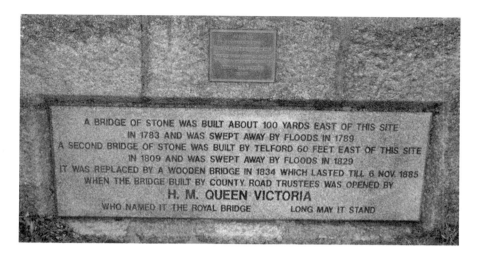

A BRIDGE OF STONE WAS BUILT ABOUT 100 YARDS EAST OF THIS SITE
IN 1783 AND WAS SWEPT AWAY BY FLOODS IN 1789
A SECOND BRIDGE OF STONE WAS BUILT BY TELFORD 60 FEET EAST OF THIS SITE
IN 1809 AND WAS SWEPT AWAY BY FLOODS IN 1829
IT WAS REPLACED BY A WOODEN BRIDGE IN 1834 WHICH LASTED TILL 6 NOV. 1885
WHEN THE BRIDGE BUILT BY COUNTY ROAD TRUSTEES WAS OPENED BY
H. M. QUEEN VICTORIA
WHO NAMED IT THE ROYAL BRIDGE   LONG MAY IT STAND

Like so many bridges on Deeside, Storm Frank in December 2015 caused major damage to the bridge. It was bombarded with tree trunks and caravans washed down the river. After thirteen weeks of painstaking work the bridge was brought back to its former glory and reopened in October 2018. The cost of the work was estimated at £450,000.

Burn of Tullich

The Burn of Tullich rises high up on Movern and rushes through a deep narrow gorge on its way to join the Dee opposite Pannanich Wells. The North Deeside Road passes over the burn a few yards west of the ruins of Tullich Church which is dedicated to St Nathalan. Before the burn reaches the Dee it is crossed by the old Deeside line, now part of the Deeside Way. There is a pool a little to the south-west of the church which has an interesting story to tell, which James Brown recounts in *The New Deeside Guide* published in 1862:

St Nathalan had committed a most awful and terrible crime that, by way of penance, he made a very heavy girdle or chain of iron which he fastened round his loins, and locked the same with a key. This key he took and threw into this pool, since called the Key Pool, saying that if he ever he found the key again, he would consider it a sign from heaven that his great and unspeakable crime was forgiven.
We are told that on a pilgrimage to Italy he caught a fish and in its stomach was a key which opened the girdle. This miracle earned him the reputation for piety and devoutness for which he was known ever after as Saint Nathalan. The key is part of the arms of the Burgh of Ballater and also those of the Ballater Highland Games.

Gordon Bridge at Cambus O' May

Prior to 1905 a ferry had to be used to cross the river. It was upstream from the railway station at Old Ferry Inn now known as Cutaway Cottage. When the railway was built the north-east corner of the cottage gable was demolished to allow trains to pass. The ferry went out of use in 1905 when a suspension bridge was built, providing access to the railway for passengers from the south side of the river. The bridge was paid for mainly from the estate of Alexander Gordon who, during his lifetime, had met the cost of the Polhollick Bridge up-river from Ballater.

The bridge was of very similar design to the one at Polhollick and carried the plaque:

**THIS BRIDGE
WAS PRESENTED
TO THE PUBLIC BY
MR. ALEXANDER GORDON,
SOUTHWOOD,
HILDENBOROUGH, KENT
ERECTED 1905**

There was also a financial contribution from the railway company and local landowners. The bridge was built by James Abernethy & Co. of Aberdeen.

Allachy Bridge

Douglas Harper in his book *River, Railway and Ravine* published in 2015 records that perusal of the maps of Glen Tanar dated 1868 and 1901 showed that eight footbridges appeared across the Water of Tanar and Water of Allachy (a tributary of the Tanar) between these dates. In examination of what remained of these bridges there was good evidence that they had been built by John Harper & Co.

Tanar Bridge

There are many footbridges and stone bridges in the estate dating from the time of Cunliffe Brooks. Two older stone bridges are worthy of special mention. The bridge of Tanar, also known as Braeloine bridge, is a hump backed bridge and could have been a military bridge. It is the bridge which takes the Fir Mounth from Tarfside in Glenesk over the Tanar. There is no evidence whatsoever that it was the work of General Wade as has been claimed. General Wade had nothing to do with the building of any road or bridge in Aberdeenshire.

G M Fraser, writing in the *Deeside Field* in 1925, suggests it dates from 1752-54 and gave access to the military road to Glen Gairn, Corgarff and by way of the Lecht to Fort George and Inverness. Today the bridge provides access across the Tanar to St Lesmo's chapel built in 1871.

Bridge of Ess

of 1752. Fenton Wyness in his book *Royal Valley* suggest that these three bridges gave rise to the couplet:

Bloodthirsty Dee she needs three;
Hungry Don he needs one!

In pagan times the Dee and the Don were regarded as having twin river gods - the Dee god being Devana who was female and the Don having the male god Devona. The belief was that the gods had to be pacified by human sacrifices, namely drownings and that the meaning of the verse was that the Dee had to claim three victims in respect of her three bridges whereas the Don insisted on only one for the Brig O' Balgownie in Old Aberdeen. Edward I of England, the Hammer of the Scots, with his army of 30,000 men and 5000 mail-clad knights camped here overnight on 2 August 1296 (according to W Douglas Simpson, the noted Aberdeen historian and one-time Librarian of Aberdeen University (though some sources give the date of a week later) and consumed a year's supply of food and drink in a single day, leaving the villagers with nothing. Jim Doig in his book *The History of Kincardine O' Neil* records the event in the poem:

O' followers he haed a flock,
Left neither capon, hen nor cock,
Na, nor butter, bread, nor cheese,
Else my informant tells me lees,
An' warst o' a' I'm wae to tell,
They left them neither maut nor ale.

Eight years later on 17 October 1304, along with his army, Edward once again visited Kincardine O' Neil before returning south by the Cairn O' Mounth. Before Edward I passed this way, other kings of Scotland had visited. On 14 August 1057 Malcolm Canmore, later to become King Malcolm III, spent a night here along with a small army of men including Macduff, his right hand man. Macbeth had come to the throne of Scotland after murdering King Duncan in 1040. Malcolm, his son, was now seeking revenge and the following morning marched north to seek out the King. They met up with Macbeth near Lumphanan where battle ensued and we are told that Malcolm killed the King. The following verse is taken from the *Wyntoun Original Chronicles*:

Oure the Mounth, thai chast him then
Rycht to the wod of Lumfanan,
Thus Makbeth slew thai than
In to the wode of Lumfanan.

The crown did not pass directly to Malcolm but first to Macbeth's son Lulach, before Malcolm became king the following year. This is the true version of the story of Macbeth and not the fictional one of Shakespeare's play.

King David I and his army forded the river here in 1150 when he was on his way north to Moray to gain better control for the crown of that part of Scotland and in 1526 King James V also passed this way. He often travelled his kingdom in disguise to see for himself the living conditions of his subjects. It is said that he stopped here for the night, staying at the croft of a family named Cochran. So hospitable were they that the King granted them tenure of the land and to this day there is a house named Cochran's Croft in the village.

A ferry crossed the river 300 metres upstream from the ford. Fenton Wyness records that it was still in use as late as 1937. It ended when a flood wrecked the boat and it was washed away. By this time the fare was 2d and the last crossing of the day was made at 10 pm.

The history of the village is kept alive in street names - Canmore Place and the new development of Durward Gardens.

Potarch Bridge

POTARCH BRIDGE NEAR BANCHORY.

The Deeside Railway from Banchory to Aboyne was completed by 1859 and it crossed the Beltie burn over a five span viaduct at Balnacraig. It was a major piece of engineering and took two years to build. Although the Deeside line was closed in 1966, it was not until 1989 that the viaduct was demolished, despite local efforts to see it preserved. It had been expected that it would take a week to complete the job but when the first arch across the Tornaveen road was taken down, the others fell like a set of dominoes. Within half-an-hour the viaduct had fallen and the famous landmark was no more.

Bridge of Beltie

The Beltie Burn flooded in 1799, 1829, 1872 and 1876, affecting the railway (closed in 1966) and damaging bridges. The road below the bridge from Glassel to Banchory is liable to serious flooding and must be used with care at times of bad weather.

Bridge of Canny

In George Robertson's *A General View of the Agriculture of Kincardineshire* first published in 1807, the Canny is described *as a considerable stream which rises from the Hill of Fare, near the western boundary of the county and passing through the highly improved lands of Glasel, where it becomes for a short space the boundary between the counties, it turns at last to the eastward, and near the house of Inchmarlo, falls into the Dee at Invercanny.*

Close to the Bridge of Canny was the site of a bobbin mill which is shown on both the first and second edition Ordnance Survey maps. Water power of the Canny burn was used to power the machinery. The mill was run by James and John Brebner from 1875 until 1887 when they transferred their business to King Street in Aberdeen. When it was closed it became a public house known as the Bobbin Mill.

The business at Bridge of Canny was taken over by James Collier. In the census of 1891 and again in 1901 his occupation and that of his three sons is listed as *bobbin maker and general wood turner.* The mills appear to have gone out of use sometime after 1905 and on the 1928 OS map the site is marked as Burnside Cottage.

In the same area was the sawmill, owned by Mr C Fraser, and also Duncan's Sawmill at Invercannie which was originally three mills - a turning mill, a meal mill and a sawmill. Later that firm branched out to manufacture cloth boards and also began making tweed. The mill was taken over by Mr J S Duthie for some years and in 1941 passed into the hands of Messrs Rosowsky and Blumstein who carried it on as a sawmill. Shortly after World War II, owing to the shortage of timber in the locality, the sawmill was forced to shut down.

Bridge of Dee at Banchory

The Bridge of Dee was built in 1798 by public subscription to replace the ferry long established at Cobleheugh, at the junction with the River Feugh where the Banchory Lodge Hotel now stands. In all probability it replaced an earlier wooden bridge which had been swept away a century earlier. Initially the new bridge was referred to as the bridge at Cobbleheugh.

In July 1829 the bridge was inspected and it was found that the wooden arch was in need of repair but before any work was done the Muckle Spate caused more damage less than a month later. Repairs were needed in 1839 when a crack in one of the piers was discovered but the state of the bridge was kept under constant review by John Smith, the Aberdeen architect, for the next ten years. In 1847 his report stated that the bridge *had a very considerable spring or shake in it when a carriage is passing along the roadway. I do not think there is any danger of it giving way from the present moderate traffic upon it.*

In 1863 John Willet, an Aberdeen civil engineer, reported to the trustees on how the existing arch could be strengthened. His solution was that diagonal bracing be introduced between the upright standards of the main girders, for the stiffening of the whole structure. When the repairs were being carried out there was a return to the ancient custom of ferrying passengers across by boat. The turnpike road trustees were responsible for the upkeep of the bridge until 1878 when they were abolished in Kincardineshire and thereafter it became the responsibility of the County Council.

It was not until the 1920s that it was found necessary to replace the central span by a cast iron central structure. By the 1970s this had become dangerous, so a temporary bailey bridge was installed.

Bridge of Dee at Banchory - 2022

In 1983 it was replaced by another temporary structure to allow work to begin on a major rebuild of the original bridge. The architect, from Grampian Regional Council Roads and Transport Department, took his inspiration from Telford's bridge at Potarch. By May 1995 the work was completed. The new reinforced concrete bridge, with fine stonework piers and arches, even has a traditional hump in the centre, something quite unknown in bridge building today.

Bridges of the Dye

The water of Dye, which is a tributary of the Feugh and in turn a tributary of the Dee, has a course of about 24 km and rises at a height of 600 metres on the south-eastern slopes of Mount Battock. It flows eastward at a fairly high altitude until it reaches the Spittal Burn on the Cairn O' Mounth. Along the way it is joined by the Water of Charr and the Builg burn.

The Cairn O' Mounth was part of the military road from Fettercairn to Fochabers and was built around 1760 under the direction of Major Caulfeild. It formalised a route that had been used by, among many others, the English army of Edward I in 1296, Macbeth on his way to defeat at the Battle of Lumphanan in 1057 and the Roman army of Julius Agricola in AD 84.

The Spittal Bridge

Nearby, centuries before, was a *spittal*, a Scottish word for a shelter for travellers. Many stories are told of things that happened in this secluded spot in these days. The road had earned the reputation as the haunt of thieves ready to rob and even kill innocent travellers, hence the need for a place of safety and for rest. Jane Geddes in her book *Deeside and the Mearns* suggests that the adjacent ruined house may well have been the spittal or perhaps more likely near the site of it.

The bridge is still used today but the parapet is regularly damaged by wide lorries. Over the years, there have been many calls to see it replaced by a bridge fit for purpose and allow the original one to be preserved.

Bridge of Dye

Bridge of Dye.

After the Spittal bridge the river turns north for the next 1.6 km to reach the Bridge of Dye, which dates from around 1680. It was built at the expense of Alexander Fraser of Durris who, at the time, owned the lands of Glen Dye. It replaced the ford which was an extremely hazardous crossing in winter.

An Act of the Scottish Parliament speaks of the *imperious waters* where many have perished. The bridge was a great asset but it did require maintenance and Alexander Fraser's factor appealed to the Scots Parliament for permission to impose tolls. Parliament granted the petition for a toll for a limited period and a charge was imposed of eight pennies for each saddle horse and rider and four pennies for each individual man or woman and each separate horse or cow, or four sheep that crossed the Bridge of Dye. But the toll proved to be very difficult to collect and the ford continued to be used except at times of spate.

In 1685 Alexander's son, Sir Peter, petitioned Parliament to have the toll made permanent but it eventually went out of use. The bridge still has the two pillars at the crown of the arch through which a chain was passed to deter travellers trying to avoid paying the toll.

Queen Victoria with Prince Albert and their daughter Alice passed this way on 21 September 1861 on her homeward journey from Fettercairn, where she had spent the night in the Ramsay Arms. In her diary she records the journey:

We came close to a very long hill, at least four miles in length, called the Cairnie Month, whence there is a very fine view; but which is entirely obscured by a heavy driving mist. We walked up part of it, and then for a while Alice and I sat alone in the carriage. We next came to the Spittal Bridge, a curious high bridge with the Dye Water to the left and the Spittal Burn to the right. Sir T. Gladstone's shooting place is close to the Bridge of Dye - where we changed carriages again, re-entering the double dog-cart with Albert.

In June 1940, as preparation for defence, the bridge was identified for planned demolition should a German invasion take place. Four months later the instruction was changed to a road block.

G J Barclay, in a paper he wrote on preparations for any attack, records that *the bridge is defended by two pillboxes built to a non standard design camouflaged as part of a granite wall running east from the B974 towards Bridge of Dye farm, forming the boundary between the farm's garden and the access track to the farm.*

In recent years the road has been realigned leaving the bridge to be better viewed. In August 1972 the bridge was given category A status.

Bridge of Bogendreip

About 6 km further down the road, the Dye flows under the picturesque bridge of Bogendreip which once again has been by passed by a new section of road. It was built in the late eighteenth century.

The Dye continues its course reaching the Feugh less than a kilometre above Strachan. Sheena Blackhall, the well known local poet and story teller, mentions Bogendreip in one of her poems:

A neep is nae culture-specific.
Tatties are fand Fae Spain tae Bogendreip.
It's nae foo ye parlez-vous that draps ye in the merde,
It's lack o thocht ahin the spukken wird.

Bridges of the Feugh

The Feugh rises in the Forest of Birse and has a course of 32 km before reaching the Dee opposite Banchory Lodge Hotel. The destruction of the Muckle Spate of 1829 is captured in the following lines of a poem by David Grant:

> *The Feugh cam' rairin' doon from Birse,*
> *An; swept the haughs o' Str'an;*
> *Horse, pigs, an kye were droont i' Dye;*
> *An' sheep by scores in A'an*

At Finzean, (pronounced *Fing-an*), on the Feugh, there are three water mills - a sawmill, turning mill and bucket mill. The power for driving these old mills is still supplied from the river and at one time it was also used to generate electricity for lighting. The sawmill dates from the 1820s and was used extensively to cut timber. It is still in use today and the mill supplied the oak flooring in the main chamber around the presiding officer's chair in the Scottish Parliament at Holyrood.

The turning mill dates from the 1830s and is still owned by the same family who built it. David Duncan is the fourth generation of his family to work in the mill and it produces timber products. The bucket mill was built in the 1850s and produces timber buckets made from staves of local Scots pine timber. It was operated by three generations of the Brown family until it was taken over by Stanley Moyes in the 1970s. Since 1999 the Birse Community Trust have been responsible for the maintenance and repairs to the Mill.

The small stream the A'an joins the Feugh at Whitestone, 3 km west of Strachan. There was a bridge here dating from 1681 but it was washed away in the Muckle Spate of 1829. The floods of 3 September 1799 are recorded in a newspaper at the time:

Since our last we have received further accounts of the damage done by the flood of the 3rd ult. The Bridge of Whitestone, over the Feugh, was carried off; and several acres of the adjoining farm the very soil was washed away, leaving nothing but gravel and stones; The Bridge lately built at Ballater shared the same fate, nothing remaining but the spring of one of the side arches. The following remarkable circumstance is related to us as authentic:- A dog belonging to a gentleman on Deeside, swam to an island where a number of sheep were pasturing, and brought eleven of them, but his strength being exhausted, the faithful animal was carried away by the flood along with the twelfth!

It took many years before a replacement, but much less grand, was built which is still to be seen today. The A'an gives its name to the parish of Strachan. The proper name of the parish is Strath-Avan which over the years was contracted in speech to Stra'an.

Strachan Bridge

At Strachan there was a wooden bridge possibly dating from the early twentieth century. It was replaced by a stone bridge in 1954. For many years, when the river was in spate, the road to the south was impassable and had to be closed. In recent years the level of the road has been raised and a series of culverts created below the road to allow flood water to pass underneath.

Feugh Lodge Suspension Bridge

FEUGH LODGE BANCHORY

Just before reaching the Bridge of Feugh there is a private suspension bridge built for Mr John Douglas of Feugh Lodge. The bridge, dating from June 1893, was supplied and erected by Louis Harper of Aberdeen.

A George Washington Wilson picture shows that the bridge at that time had an arched appearance and the pillars possibly were made of timber. These have been replaced by steel and the deck is now more or less horizontal.

Feugh Bridge

The Bridge of Feugh is one of the most photographed sights in Deeside and dates from 1790. It was built by the Russells of Blackhall to provide better access to Banchory from the south. The River Feugh can quickly turn into a dramatic torrent of water when it is swollen by rainfall on the Mounth. On 3 August 1829 the Muckle Spate flooded the old Toll House on the north bank. The river rose 7.6 metres above the ordinary level and the water was up to the parapets of the bridge. The local baker had walked along the top edge just before part of the parapet gave way. Even though the bridge had become the responsibility of the turnpike road trust in 1800, the Russell family organised and paid for the maintenance of the bridge, being reimbursed subsequently by the road trust.

The Statistical Account of Banchory-Ternan of 1842 written by the Rev
William Anderson gives an excellent description of the bridge: *A bridge of
two principal arches is thrown over the stream, just below the fall; and few
spots in the parish exhibit a more striking view than the alpine scenery of
this place, especially when the Feugh, swollen by rain, fills the whole
channel with a thundering noise, and foaming waters, sweeps through the
arches into the whirlpool below.*

The design of the old toll house at the north end of the bridge, is unique
among those on Deeside. It later became the home of John Moir, a blind
shopkeeper and local poet:

> *I keep this shop, as a' may see,*
> *In order that this shop keep me;*
> *But gin the truth I maun reveal,*
> *Nane o' the twa are keepit weel.*
> *Yet I am fain my best tae dee*
> *An' value for you bawbees gie*
> *My gratefu' thanks are due tae a'*
> *Wha gie me ony trade ava!*

The bridge has for many years been a traditional favourite spot for tourists
to visit:

> *Tae see the Feugh gang roarin' by*
> *An' watch the salmon louping*

Little has changed over the years except that there is now an ugly iron viewing platform for pedestrians which was erected in 1976. The bridge is less than 3.4 metres wide and until 1965 Strachan's familiar red buses, which used the south Deeside road, crossed the bridge on the way to Banchory.

Falls of Feugh viewing platform

In recent years, following the world craze, the footbridge saw it adorned with hundreds of padlocks known as love locks. Such was the weight of them that in 2015 the decision was taken to remove them. Instead, couples are now encouraged to take selfies next to a newly installed oak love heart sculpture.

The Slug Road and the Toll Houses and Bridges

The new bridge at Cobbleheugh and the Bridge of Feugh enabled the construction of a turnpike road from Banchory to Stonehaven. In 1799 work had begun on the road linking the Feugh and Cobbleheugh bridges. A stone, now partially hidden and covered in ivy, can be seen on the north bank of the Feugh.

Under the terms of a Parliamentary Act of 1800, the trustees met in Stonehaven for the first time on 19 May of that year. Only three attended the meeting, John Douglas of Tilquhillie, James Rose of Feughside and John Innes of Durris, described as the principal tacksman, that is the person who held the lease of the estate. At the meeting William Gordon was appointed treasurer and clerk and William Shaw, postmaster at Banchory-Ternan, was appointed surveyor and overseer. Shaw, as well as being the postmaster, was also what was known at the time as a squarewright, a Scottish term for a carpenter. The section of the road from the bridge at Cobbleheugh to the Bridge of Feugh had been completed in 1799 and it was decided that the next section should head eastwards along the existing rough road before branching south-east at Maryfield toward the higher ground. Gordon and Shaw were instructed to mark the route of the road as far as Darnford where it crossed the Burn of Sheeoch.

The building of the road was paid for by subscriptions from the trustees who were the local landowners. In addition to those mentioned above were Francis Russell of Blackhall and Sir Robert Burnett of Leys.

In December 1800 the trustees awarded a contract for widening the existing road between Cobbleheugh and Balbridie with later contracts taking the road to Darnford. Two bridges were required - one at Knappach and the other at Blairydrine and these were built under the supervision of Robert Wright, mason of Denside. Toll gates and houses were built at the Bridge of Feugh and at Darnford. Instead of appointing toll keepers the decision was taken to auction the responsibility for the collection of the tolls to the highest bidder. The gate at the Bridge of Feugh was by far the most lucrative because of its position at the junction of the Cairn O' Mounth and South Deeside road.

Three of the trustees, Francis Russell of Blackhall, John Douglas of Inchmarlo and John Innes at Durris, held a meeting at the West Boat of Durris on 1 June 1801, acknowledging the loan of £75 given by the kirk session of Durris, towards the cost of the building of the road, at which it was resolved *that such proportion of the Tolls or Duties arising in virtue of the Act for making and repairing the Road from the Town of Stonehaven , through the Slug mount, to the New Bridge over the River Dee at Cobleheugh, in the County of Kincardine, for behoof of the Poor of the parish of Durris such proportion of the Tolls or Duties, and every matter or article connected with the collection of them.* The agreement to pay a proportion of the tolls to the Durris kirk session for the benefit of the poor, was to be continued until the loan was repaid with interest of five per cent per annum. No doubt much of this initiative was the idea of the trustee, John Innes of Durris, who was the major subscriber to the cost of the road. He was the driving force, ensuring that the road, some 11 km of which passed through the estate, was completed to a high standard and according to contract. During 1802 Robert Wright took over from William Shaw the responsibility for supervising the unfinished work on the road.

It was not until December 1803 that the road was completed, following a route over the eastern fringes of the Grampian mountains climbing to at one point 230 metres above sea level, before descending to the old bridge over the Water of Cowie near Stonehaven. The Slug road gets its name from the Gaelic word *sloc* meaning hollow due to the road following a narrow *mountain pass*.
A full account of the building of the Turnpike Road, written by Thomas Day, was published by the Edinburgh University Press in *Northern Scotland* Volume 13.

Queen Victoria and Prince Albert with members of the family used the Slug road on 7 October 1851. They left by coach from Balmoral that morning and the *Illustrated London News* of 18 October reports that *on leaving Banchory the Royal couple passed the romantic bridge of Feugh, and then, turned eastward, crossed the Grampian Chain, at a place called the Slug, whence for 7 miles the drive was as cheerless, barren and wild as can well be imagined. On emerging from the Slug the Queen drove on by Ury, the seat of Captain Ramsay, towards the railway station of Stonehaven, where the Royal carriage drew up at half past one o'clock.*

Crathes was opened. This replaced the laird's private halt which was sited a short distance west of the railway bridge. When the new station was built at Crathes the old halt was no longer required but a condition of the feu charter, granted to the railway company for the building of the public station, was that all trains should stop at Crathes. When the railway closed in 1966 the track was removed leaving only the structure of the old bridge.

Perhaps the most interesting bridge is the old pack horse bridge with its low parapets. It is one of the few that remain in Scotland and possibly dates from around 1700. It never was a bridge used by wheeled carriages, which were late to arrive in this part of the country.

Durris Bridge at Crathes

The old Durris bridge was built in 1862 by Alexander Mactier, a wealthy East India merchant, then proprietor of Durris, to provide access from Durris to Crathes station. In earlier days there was a ford and later a ferry at Balbridie providing a route from Tilquhillie castle on the south bank to Crathes castle on the north. While the bridge was under construction the Dee flooded twice causing the coffer dam - the watertight enclosure pumped dry to permit work to be carried out beneath the water line - to be breached. Although Mactier bore the whole cost of the bridge he was recouped to some extent by a charge for its use. The reason he gave was that his tenants who used the Park bridge, to the east, were already paying a toll and it was only fair to levy a charge on his tenants who used the new bridge. This charge, however, soon fell into abeyance.

In 1977 a new wider bridge was built and the road re-aligned. The centre pillar of the old bridge can still be seen downstream from the new crossing. In 2017 the bridge had to be closed for a period for essential maintenance.

On a plaque on the east parapet of the bridge is the following inscription:

ERECTED 1862
DURRIS BRIDGE
DESIGNED BY
JOHN WILLET, ESQRE C.E
ABERDEEN

CONTRACTORS.
SMITH AND DEY
BUILDERS DURRIS
JAMES TOD AND SON
ENGINEERS
EDINBURGH

Sheeoch Bridges

Cryne's Cross Mounth, from Fordoun to Durris, was in the Middle Ages an important crossing and those that used this route would ford the Dee and later the ferry at the Mills of Drum.

W Douglas Simpson notes, in an article he wrote in 1928 for the *Society of Antiquaries of Scotland*, that in the thirteenth century the Dee may have been spanned by a wooden bridge at Durris but there is no confirmative evidence. In the reign of Alexander III during the same century, it was recorded that repairs were made to a bridge at Dores, the original spelling of Durris. The bridge referred to might have been the drawbridge at Durris castle.

Kirkton of Durris was an important site along the route to Aberdeen from the south. In 1296 Edward I, along with his 35,000 troops, crossed to Durris by way of Cryne's Cross Mounth. He spent the night at Durris castle, *the manour among the mountains.* The following day he left for Aberdeen to consolidate his possession of Scotland.

The Sheeoch burn rises in the foothills of Kerloch and joins the Dee at Kirkton of Durris. As well as the road bridge on the South Deeside road there are four others that cross the burn further upstream - Blairydrine, Wardend, Belladrum and Kirkton.

Blairydrine Bridge

The Blairydine bridge crosses the Sheeoch close to where the road from Strachan meets the Slug and dates from 1796 with further work in 1802 as part of the roads construction under the supervision of Robert Wright, mason of Denside.

The farm of Blairydrine is a short distance from where the bridge now stands and in 1478 it was part of the barony of Dores (Durris) and owned by William Keith, 2nd Earl Marischal. His tenant of the property was Andrew Hog, who had come from Scandinavia to settle in Kincardineshire.

King James V often travelled incognito around his kingdom and in October 1537 he and his party, having forded the Dee at the Mills of Drum, were caught in a violent thunderstorm and were given shelter at the farm of Blairydrine. He was given generous hospitality by the then tenant farmer, Monane Hog who, unaware of the King's identity, slaughtered several hogs to serve at the King's table. The King was so impressed with his generosity that he later granted the farm and the lands to the family. The family prospered and in the *Statistical Account of Durris* written in 1838 it is recorded that in 1787 an Alexander Hog had left £5 per annum for the salary of the teacher of a school under the patronage of the kirk session of Durris. The school was known as *Mr Hog's Charity School* and the teacher was required to teach gratis ten poor children recommended by the kirk session.

Wardend

The burn at Wardend is wider at this point and the number of flat stones perhaps indicate that there was once a ford here and later a wooden bridge. At one time there was a school at Burnside, adjacent to the farm at Wardend, and the story is told how the dominie, on one stormy night, crossed the wooden bridge to the farm to collect milk and on his return the bridge collapsed and he was drowned. An embellished account says that he had his dog with him and it suffered the same fate. The present bridge probably dates from around 1800.

Belladrum Bridge

The Belladrum (also spelt Balladrum) bridge was paid for by Thomas Fraser. Robin Jackson in his book, *The Parish of Durris,* records that in his will Thomas Fraser left forty pounds for the building of a stout bridge and seven pounds for its maintenance. Thomas Fraser was a judge advocate and chaplain and served on HMS Sussex which sank in the straits of Gibraltar in 1694. The bridge was built by the turn of the century and to meet the terms of his bequest it has his name and coat of arms on a plaque on the stonework. In 2022 the plaque was cleaned but the lettering was too eroded to reveal the inscription.

Belladrum Bridge in Durris

Old Bridge of Sheeoch at Kirkton of Durris

The Kirkton bridge is located a short distance upstream from the South Deeside road. It has existed here for centuries and until 2000 was an important crossing for the people of Kirkton as the road bridge on the South Deeside road was considered unsafe for pedestrians. In 2000 the Friends of Durris Forest noted that part of the bridge had fallen away and there was risk of a major collapse. Dunecht Estates, owners of the land, were contacted but were not prepared to offer resources for restoration. Aberdeenshire Council, aware of the condition of the bridge, commissioned a structural report in late 2001.

The report advised that the bridge was dangerous and could collapse at any time. With no help from Aberdeenshire Council or Historic Scotland, the Friends of Durris Forest began searching for other funding but unfortunately a recent violent storm has now destroyed a substantial portion of the bridge. It is hoped that as part of architectural heritage, the bridge can still be saved and used once again by the people of Kirkton of Durris.

Park Bridge

A road linking the Deeside turnpike via the Park Bridge to the parish of Durris was laid out by the Deeside Railway Company in order to encourage passengers and freight from the south side.

A metal plate on the south-west girder of the bridge reads:

James Abernethy & Co., Ferryhill Foundry, Aberdeen, 1854.

Pontage of one half-penny for a foot passenger, one penny for a passenger with a bicycle and three pence for a motor car was charged for the use of the bridge and was the last toll bridge in use in Aberdeenshire. The toll house on the north bank can still be seen. British Rail continued to collect the tolls right up to the mid 1950s. In April 1971 the bridge was given category A status.

On a wooded mound on the south end of the bridge is an octagonal tower (erroneously called Keith's Tower), erected in 1825 by the Duke of Gordon to commemorate his acquisition of the estate of Durris after a protracted lawsuit. It was on the north bank of the river in an area still known as Keith's Muir that in the fourteeenth century, a fierce engagement took place between the Irvines of Drum and the Keiths, Great Marischals of Scotland who had estates on the south bank. Victory went to the Irvines but the marriage of Alexander, son of Sir Alexander Irvine, who was killed at the Battle of Harlaw in 1411, to Elizabeth Keith, daughter of the then Great Marischal, brought the feud to an end.

In 2002 this spirit of friendship was further marked by a ceremony which took place on the bridge between Michael Keith, 13th Earl of Kintore,

chief of the Clan Keith and David Irvine, Laird of Drum 26th chief of
Irvine of Drum.

Photo © Leopard Magazine

Park Bridge has been closed to all vehicles since February 2019 after a
routine inspection found serious defects. Drivers have been faced with a
13km diversion. There has been no date given for work to be undertaken to
allow for a possible reopening and the situation has become increasingly
tense with the local residents.

Tilbouries Bridges

The current road bridge carries the South Deeside road across a gorge cut
by the Tilbouries burn which joins the Dee nearby. This replaced an earlier
bridge which was on a sharp bend a short distance upstream.

The Romans came to Deeside, using the Elsick Mounth as their route, in
around AD 210 when the Roman Emperor Septimius Severus forded the
river at Tilbouries. A full account of the Roman arrival is contained in an
article written by John Stuart of Inchbreck for the *Society of Antiquaries of
Scotland* published in 1822:

The Roman army having marched (from Raedykes near Stonehaven) *about
12 miles arrived at the banks of the Dee at a place called Tilbouries about
7 or 8 miles from Aberdeen where there still appears a broad, shallow and
excellent ford, and pitched camp on a rising ground on the opposite bank.
This is now called Normandykes which has probably been corrupted in the
course of time from Roman dykes and which until late supposed to be a
camp of the Danes or Norwegians. On the south side the stones on the
barren heath appear to be vitrified by fire but below not. It might be*

supposed that the Romans burned the woods growing here to open up a passage for their army. In 1807 a detailed survey by the author (John Stuart of Inchbreck) *accompanied by Irvine of Drum and Capt Henderson of the 29th regiment of foot made a drawing of Normandykes and believed it to be Roman.*

It has been suggested that the Romans may have, with their great engineering skills, built a solid passage across the river for their men, beasts and baggage or even a wooden bridge. Today, any trace of where the ford might have been is hard to find. It has been suggested that it may have disappeared during World War II as part of our defences should a German invasion have occurred. In the 1970s a British Gas Corporation pipeline was laid, which crossed the Dee at this point finally obliterating any remaining traces.

Tilbouries current road bridge

Tilbouries old road bridge

Maryculter bridge

But a road bridge was never built at Cults.

The *Aberdeen Free Press* on 14 September carried an account of the opening and very unusual for the time, carried a picture of the bridge. The area around the bridge has, over the years, been prone to flooding. The culvert under the bridge was found to be inadequate when the river was in spate. On 25 January 1937, for example, the roadway of the bridge was under 1.2 metres of water and ten years later the Aberdeen in-shore lifeboat had to be used to rescue people from their flooded homes, especially in the caravan site nearby.

The bridge is now dwarfed by the opening, in late 2018, of the new crossing of the river as part of the Aberdeen bypass.

Heathcot Ferry

Bella's last ferry crossing

Hidden and unnoticed on the bridge is heraldry belonging to organisations within the city and county area. The arms are carved from Rubislaw granite and are as follows:

On the upstream side of the bridge from the Kincorth side (South) to the Duthie Park bank (North):

The County of Kincardine
The University of Aberdeen
Robert Gordon's College, Aberdeen
The County of Aberdeen

On the downstream side of the bridge from the Kincorth side (South) to the Duthie Park bank (North):

Aberdeen Harbour Board of Commissioners
Aberdeen Grammar School
The Incorporated Trades of Aberdeen
The City & Royal Burgh of Aberdeen

Four shield-bearing lions were planned to sit on the parapet for further embellishment. Work on them was held up by the war and eventually the Town Council voted against continuing the work.

Today we can see the partially completed sculptures in Hazlehead Park with the plaque.

Note that on the plaque the designer of the bridge is given as *Sir Frank Mearns* but it should read **Mears**. The bridge opened in the dark days of war and we are told it had telegraph poles and wires installed on it but they were not what they seemed. In fact, they were part of the city's defences to prevent enemy planes landing on the dual carriageway.

The approach to the bridge from the north by way of Great Southern road was lined with handsome cast iron lamp standards with the arms of the city of Aberdeen and were designed by Frank C Mears. At a later date, at the suggestion of the Aberdeen artist Eric Auld, the arms were painted and gilded, displaying part of the heritage of the city. A number of the old lamp standards have now been replaced with more modern equivalents. At the time of the opening the road linking Kincorth and Tullos to the south was still to be completed.

Queen Elizabeth Bridge

In the early 1980s work began to replace the Wellington suspension bridge by one more suitable for the increase in traffic. What was built was a fairly typical three-span concrete bridge with a dual carriageway and pavements across the river. The cost of the bridge was £5.7 million which included a grant of £1.15 million from the European Union.

In 1983 the bridge was completed and it was very appropriate that this, the newest bridge over the Dee, should be formally opened by Her Majesty The Queen the following year.

The Queen arrived on the morning of the formal opening aboard *HMY Britannia* to start her annual holiday at Balmoral. She was accompanied by HRH Princess Margaret and was welcomed by the Lord Lieutenant of Aberdeen Henry Rae. Before inviting the Queen to formally open the bridge, Grampian Region's Convener, John Sorrie, spoke of the new addition to *Aberdeen's Royal Family of Bridges.*

The name could not be more appropriate with King George VI bridge upstream and within sight downstream the Queen Victoria bridge.

Before unveiling the plaque HM The Queen said she was delighted to follow family tradition by giving her name to the new bridge and continued *the river it spans is one I have known all my life and it occupies a special place in the affections of myself and my family.*

The inscription on the plaque reads:

HER MAJESTY THE QUEEN

ON 10th AUGUST 1984 UNVEILED THIS PLAQUE

TO COMMEMORATE THE COMPLETION OF

THE QUEEN ELIZABETH BRIDGE

BUILT BY GRAMPIAN REGIONAL COUNCIL

The Estuary of the River

For centuries the estuary of the river was wide and shallow and with sandbanks at low tide. The river entered from the south west on a northerly course before turning eastwards towards the sea, with many channels and islets, known as the *inches*. The channels were also fed by the Denburn, Millburn and Powcreek burn further to the east. It has been likened to have been a miniature version of the Amazon delta. On the north bank of the estuary is an area known quite incorrectly as Footdee. While it cannot be denied that it is at the Foot of the Dee, the name is derived from St Fittick, a saint who, we are told, preached to the fisher folk in the area.

The Denburn which rises near Kingwells is joined by the Gilcomstoun burn on its course of 8 km and may well be the origin of the name of Aberdeen. Ptolemy's map in his *System of Geography* drawn in AD 146, as well as marking Deva fluvius, which is interpreted as the river Dee, shows Vacomagi which was the name given by the Romans to the people who lived in *Caledonia. Devana* is also marked which is said to mean *the town of two waters* which many historians claim is Aberdeen, with its two rivers of the Dee and Don. In 1153 the name *Apardion* appears in an account of a voyage of the son of a Norwegian king who *spread his sails to the south and brought his ships to the town of Apardion where he killed many people and wasted the city.* It is thought that *Apardion* was Aberdeen. Apardion is derived from two words *aber,* the mouth of a river and *da-awin* meaning *two streams* - interpreted as the rivers Dee and Don. But today many claim that Aberdeen derives its name from the two streams of Denburn and the Gilcomstoun burn. Very little of the Denburn is visible today as over the years much of it has been culverted to allow for the expansion of the city.

It is interesting that both the Roman *Devana* and Norwegian *Apardion* are still remembered in Aberdeen. With a slight alteration of spelling, Devana gave its name to the Devanha Brewery and Distillery which was situated on Riverside Drive downstream from the railway bridge. The business finally closed in 1915 after eighty years of trading. Devanha continues in street names in Ferryhill and several businesses in the city have Apardion as part of their name.

Changing the Course of the River

Aberdeen harbour was established in 1136 by King David I of Scotland and it is believed to be the oldest in Britain with a history spanning nearly a thousand years. According to the *Guinness Book of Records*, Aberdeen Harbour and its predecessors represent the oldest continuous commercial business in the United Kingdom.

It was not until 1781 that the north pier was constructed by John Smeaton to prevent drifting sand impeding the estuary but it required regular repair and extensive dredging. In 1801 Thomas Telford was commissioned to provide a scheme for improvement of the harbour but it was not until the passing of the Aberdeen Harbour Act of 1868 that the Harbour Commissioners agreed on a scheme to divert the river Dee to the south. By that time Aberdeen had become an increasingly expanding city with a harbour not adequate to deal with its trade and fishing industry. The first turf was cut by Lord Provost William Leslie on 22 December 1869. Most of the work was carried out by manual labour using picks and shovels.

There was no official inauguration of the new channel but the river was following its more southerly channel we see today, by the beginning of 1873. The diversion of the Dee allowed an enlarging of the harbour area creating the Albert Quay, a further dock and quayside, but ironically much of the old fish village of Torry was lost by the change of course of the river.

Victoria Bridge

The Aberdeen Burgh Records of 1648 refer to a ferry at the entrance to the harbour for travellers wanting or calling a boat from Torry and later, to an upper ferry at Ferryhill. In 1871 John Harper, who at the time was a member of Aberdeen Town Council, offered, at his own expense, to build one of his suspension bridges across the Dee in the line of what is now South Market Street but this was declined by the Council. However, all that was to change.

Wednesday 5 April 1876 was a sacramental feast day and it had become the custom for people in Aberdeen to cross by ferry from Pocra Quay to Torry to enjoy the fair held there and enjoy the countryside around Nigg. People were waiting at each side and had become impatient waiting for the ferry to arrive. When it did, they rushed to get on without giving time for passengers to disembark. The boat set off heavily overloaded with more than 70 passengers. All on board were thrown into the water when the boat capsized and 32 of the passengers were drowned.

The Board of Trade enquiry, following the disaster, attributed blame on the police, the over-laden boat and a poorly spliced rope on the pulley wheel. Alexander Kennedy, the tacksman (the leasee) of the ferry, was charged with culpable homicide and neglect of duty but he never went to trial. He drank himself to death, passing away in January 1877 some ten months before the trial was due to take place. All this led to the demands for a safer form of transport across the river and hence the building of the Victoria Bridge. The bridge was not to be a suspension bridge but a substantial road bridge. It was designed by Edward Blyth and built by John Fyfe using Kemnay granite. The roadway originally was laid with granite cassies for better wear from the wheels of carts crossing the bridge. It was completed at a cost of £15,000 and opened on 2 July 1881 by the Lord Provost of Aberdeen, Peter Esslemont.

The bridge provided a shorter link between the harbour and Torry than the Wellington chain bridge completed further up-stream in 1830. It also carried gas and water services across the river to Torry. At that time Torry was part of Kincardineshire and had, in its own right, been a Royal Burgh since 1495. It was not until 1891 that it became a suburb of Aberdeen.

Somewhat belatedly, a plaque was unveiled in February 2005 when children from Torry primary schools, dressed as the victims of the ferry boat disaster, walked across the bridge prior to a service being held to remember those who lost their lives.

> **VICTORIA BRIDGE**
>
> Erected following the Dee Ferry Boat Disaster, which claimed the lives of 32 people on 5April 1876. Formally opened 2 July 1881. It was partly funded by public contribution.
> The link provided by the bridge allowed direct access for carriages from Torry, via Market Street, to the heart of Aberdeen.
>
> **CITY OF ABERDEEN**

Conclusion

This book has covered all the bridges of the Dee and some on the main tributaries. There are so many bridges on the many tributaries and the authors have limited their selection to those that have a story to tell.

Will any new bridges be constructed across the river?
In 2013 there was a proposal to provide a footbridge across the Dee at Braemar. The idea was that such a crossing would link Braemar directly with tracks to the Cairngorms and would be a boost for the local community. It did not meet with favour by all and so far, it remains just an idea.

In 2017 the Aberdeen and Grampian Chamber of Commerce set up a group to come up with ideas to revitalise the city of Aberdeen. One of the suggestions was to build a cable car between the Castlegate and Nigg Bay which would have crossed high above the river Dee. Architect Chris Smith, who worked for Davidson Smith Partnership, came up with the concept. He said: *With the new south harbour soon to open and the cruise ships on their way, we feel this is a huge opportunity to bring thousands of people directly into the Castlegate, on a new and exciting, sustainable mode of transport, as a way to rejuvenate the area, including Union Street, through increased footfall.*

Will either of these ambitious projects ever become new bridges of the Dee? There is no doubt that, because of the age of many of the existing bridges, regular maintenance and occasional major repairs will be necessary, if we want to ensure that they retain their important contribution to the heritage of this part of Scotland.

Further Reading

Many books have been written in praise of Royal Deeside. However, the author has found the following of particular interest and recommends them to those who wish to explore the area further. They are listed in chronological order of original publication dates.

The Great Moray Floods, Sir Thomas Dick Lauder	Published 1830
A Guide to the Highlands of Deeside, James Brown	Published 1831[1]
Natural History of the Dee, William Macgillivray	Published 1855
Deeside Tales, John Grant Michie	Published 1872
The Scenery of the Dee, Gibb and Hay	Published 1884
Deeside, Alex. McConnochie	Published 1893[2]
History of the Valley of the Dee, John Mackintosh	Published 1895
Dictionary of Deeside, James Coutts	Published 1899
The Deeside Guide, author unknown	Published 1891
Deeside, Robert Anderson	Published 1911
The Old Deeside Road, G M Fraser.	Published 1921[3]
Royal Valley, Fenton Wyness.	Published 1968
Portrait of Aberdeen & Deeside, Cuthbert Graham	Published 1972
The Military Roads in Scotland, William Taylor	Published 1976
Royal Deeside, John S Smith	Published 1984
Valley of the Dee, Robert Smith	Published 1989
Scenery of the Dee, Jim Henderson	Published 2000
Glentanar Valley of Echoes, Pierre Fouin	Published 2009
The Old Deeside Road Revisited, Graham J Marr	Published 2014
River, Railway and Ravine, Douglas Harper	Published 2015

1 A later edition with the title *The New Deeside Guide*, was published in 1862. It was only in 1869, three years after his death, that it was discovered that the author was Joseph Robertson who had written the guide at the age of 21, whilst on holiday in Ballater.
2 Republished by EP Publishing, 1972
3 Republished by Robin Callander, 1980

Acknowledgements

Several people and organisations have kindly offered their assistance and resources during the writing of this book. These include:
Colin Blackhall, Gordon Casely, Douglas Harper, Robin Jackson, John Reid and The Cairngorm Club

Photo Credits

For most part, old postcards have been used to populate the text with visual content. Where this has not been possible, images have been used under Creative Commons License or with consent. We are very grateful to these individuals for their permission.

Andy73	Burn o' Vat
John Aldersey-Williams	Spittal Bridge
Jim Barton	Quoich Bridge
Anne Burgess	Coy and AWP bridges
Dorothy Carse	Daldownie Bridge
Gordon Casely	Lui footbridge and Brunel Bridges
Nigel Corby	Strachan Bridge
Stephen Craven	Queen Elizabeth Bridge
Alan Findlay	Allachy, Old Sheeoch and Tilbouries bridges
Keith Grinstead	Cambus o' May suspension bridge - damaged
Stanley Howe	Balmoral Suspension, Blairydrine, Cattie, Kincardine o' Neil, Feugh footbridge, Danzig, Bogendreip and Culter bridges.
G Laird	Gairnshiel, Ey and Girnock bridges
Robin Jackson	Belladrum Bridge
Leopard Magazine	Irvine and Keith clan chiefs
Ian Mitchell	Old Military Bridge in Glen Clunie
John Reid	Feugh stone, Bellfield House and Park bridge
Ewen Rennie	Maryculter Bridge
Tom Richardson	White Bridge
Colin Smith	Dinnie stones at Potarch
Mike Stephen	Society Bridge and Invercauld Bridge
Robert Struthers	Lui and Polhollick Bridges
The Cairngorm Club	Corrour and Canadian Bridges
Peter Ward	St Devenick's Bridge
Andrew Wood	Tanar Bridge

The Authors

Stewart Wilson, retired Rector of Banchory
Academy, is the life-long recorder of events,
people and the history of Deeside.
He has produced a history of Cunard Line
illustrated in stamps and old postcards part of
which is on view in the libraries of the Cunard
ships.
Stewart has given a lifetime of service to the Scout
Movement and has been a Rotarian for over 40
years. His other interests include the preservation

of the historic huts of the early explorers of Antarctica, maps of
Kincardineshire and Robert Burns.

Chris Engel is a retired oil industry geologist and
former local business owner. He was founding
secretary and then chairman of the Grampian
Transport Museum. Chris is lead voluntary mentor
on a successful STEM Greenpower project at
Banchory Academy. He has been a member of
Rotary for over 20 years.
His interests include local history, genealogy, gold
prospecting, metal detecting and travel adventure.
Although he has written magazine articles in the past, this is his first
experience of compiling a book.

We welcome comments and corrections
bridges@crathes.com

Printed in Great Britain
by Amazon

80095038R00078